NO LONGER PROPERTY OF
SEATTLE PUBLIC LIBRARY

South Park

AUG 03 2016

Branch

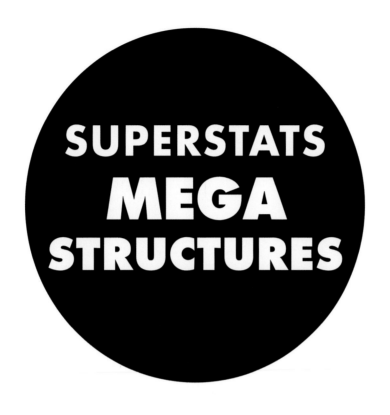

SUPERSTATS
MEGA
STRUCTURES

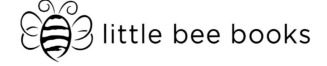

little bee books

little bee books

A division of Bonnier Publishing
853 Broadway, New York, New York 10003

Project managed and commissioned by Dynamo Limited
    Author: Helen Greathead
    Editor/Picture research: Dynamo Limited
    Design: Dynamo Limited
    Index: Marie Lorimer

Copyright © 2016 by Weldon Owen. This little bee books edition, 2016.

All rights reserved, including the right of reproduction in whole or in part in any form.

LITTLE BEE BOOKS is a trademark of Bonnier Publishing Group, and associated colophon is a trademark of Bonnier Publishing Group.

Manufactured in China [025]

Printed in Guang Dong, China

First Edition: 10 9 8 7 6 5 4 3 2 1

Library of Congress Cataloging-in-Publication Data is available upon request.

ISBN: 978-1-4998-0241-2

littlebeebooks.com

bonnierpublishing.com

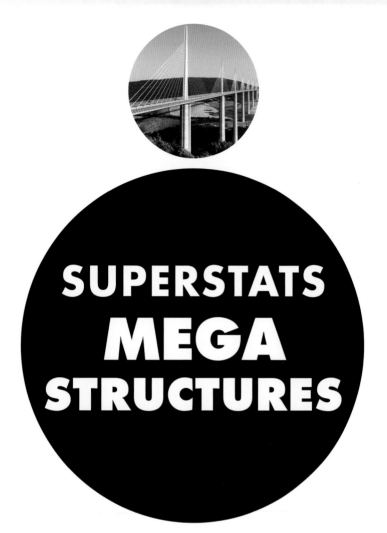

SUPERSTATS
MEGA
STRUCTURES

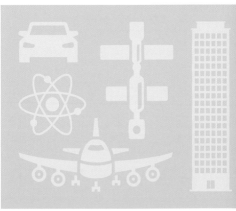

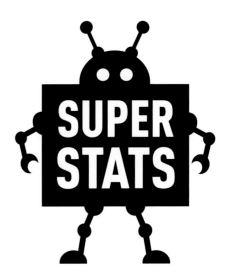

CONTENTS

TALL WALLS

The Great Wall of China is the longest structure ever built by man. It runs across northern China and was designed to keep out unfriendly neighbors. The wall doesn't stretch in one long line; sometimes two walls run side by side.

THE GREAT WALL OF CHINA

THE PATHS WERE MADE WIDE ENOUGH TO CARRY TEN SOLDIERS OR FIVE HORSES SIDE BY SIDE

THE WALLS STAND 26 FT. TALL IN PLACES

MORTAR WAS MADE FROM CLAY, LIME, AND RICE FLOUR

🐞 FACT FILE

▲ Chinese provinces began building walls of earth and stone for protection from each other in the seventh century BCE.

▲ In 221 BCE the different provinces of China were brought together under China's first Emperor, Shihuangdi, in the Qin Dynasty. Earlier walls were linked to create one long wall.

▲ Improvements and extensions to the wall continued for more than 2,000 years!

▲ The newest parts of the wall were built in the Ming Dynasty, which ended in the seventeenth century.

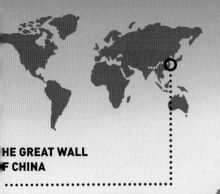

HE GREAT WALL F CHINA

WATCHTOWERS WERE BUILT SO THAT SIGNALS COULD BE SENT FROM ONE TO THE OTHER, USING FLAGS OR SMOKE

In the 1950s, Chinese leader Mao Zedong allowed people to take down parts of the wall and use the bricks to build houses and farms.

Millions of men were involved in building the wall, including criminals and peasants.

The wall is nicknamed "the longest cemetery on Earth," because so many workers died there, from hunger and being overworked.

IT'S A RECORD!

13,170 MILES LONG

The official total length of the Great Wall of China.

^ THE BERLIN WALL

The Great Wall cannot be seen from the moon.

70%

All that remains of the original wall today.

GREAT **WALLS**

◢ **THE BERLIN WALL**

The Berlin Wall was built after World War II to stop people escaping from East to West Germany. In total, it was 96 miles long, but it was demolished in the 1990s.

◢ **HADRIAN'S WALL**

It took 18,000 soldiers and 4.4 million tons of stone to build Hadrian's Wall in England, which protected the northwest edge of the Roman Empire and stretched 73 miles.

◢ **WALLS OF BABYLON**

Ancient walls built around Babylon (now in Iraq) in around 600 BCE were said to be well over 40 ft. high and wide enough to allow a chariot drawn by four horses to turn around.

Parts of the Great Wall in the desert were built using sand, branches, and decayed plants.

8,000,000

<<<<<<<<<<<<<<

The number of visitors to the Great Wall in just one day during a Chinese holiday in 2014.

SCRAPING THE SKY

Up until the middle of the nineteenth century, the tallest structures in the world were mostly built of stone. Things changed when new materials and safe elevators meant all sorts of buildings could reach for the sky.

BURJ KHALIFA

When the Burj Khalifa was officially opened in Dubai, United Arab Emirates, in 2010, it was the tallest building in the world. It measures a record-breaking 2,717 feet tall.

FACT FILE

BUILDING FACTS

▲ The Burj Khalifa took three years to complete, with two years spent fitting aluminum, stainless steel, and glass cladding to the outside of the building.

▲ **11,653,840 CUBIC FEET** of concrete was used in its construction.

▲ **4,400 TONS** of steel was used to support its telescopic spire.

▲ **12,000** employees worked on the build each day.

▲ **22 MILLION** hours of labor were spent on the building.

BURJ KHALIFA, DUBAI, UNITED ARAB EMIRATES

HIGHEST POINT: 2,717 FT.

THE TEMPERATURE AT THE TOP IS 15°F COOLER THAN AT THE ENTRANCE ON THE GROUND FLOOR

LEVEL 143: THE WORLD'S HIGHEST NIGHTCLUB

LEVEL 124: OBSERVATION DECK

Take the elevator from the bottom of the Burj at sunset, then ride to the viewing platform 60 seconds up, and you can see the sunset twice!

2018

In 2018, the Kingdom Tower in Jeddah, Saudi Arabia, is due to be completed. The building will be 3,281 ft. tall. That's over 550 ft. taller than the Burj!

In January 2010, the Burj hosted the world's highest over firework display.

LEVELS 8 TO 38: THE ARMANI HOTEL

AND SWIMMING POOLS, GYMS, A LIBRARY, AND A SHOP

TOP TOWERS

At 1,483 ft. tall, the Petronas Towers in Kuala Lumpur, Malaysia, is the tallest twin building in the world. The towers are connected with a glass bridge at a height of 558 ft.

IT'S A RECORD!

3,314 *FEET PER MINUTE*

The speed of the world's fastest elevator, in Taiwan's Taipei 101 building. It takes just 37 seconds to ride from the 5th to the 89th floor.

LEVEL 76: THE WORLD'S SECOND-HIGHEST SWIMMING POOL (INDOOR AND OUTDOOR)

DESERT FLOWER

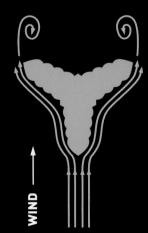

WIND →

The Burj's Y-shaped layout was inspired by a desert flower called the spider lily. The shape provides protection from desert storms, and means more rooms have views.

19 DAYS

The time it took to build the 57-floor Mini Sky City in China in 2015

UNSINKABLE!

At the beginning of the twentieth century, people really believed in new technology. So, when the RMS *Titanic*—the world's largest, most luxurious passenger ship ever—set sail, nobody thought it could possibly sink.

LOCATION WHERE THE *TITANIC* SANK, OFF THE COAST OF NEWFOUNDLAND, CANADA

FACT FILE

TITANIC STATISTICS

▲ The *Titanic* was built by Harland and Wolff at Queen's Island in Belfast Harbour, Northern Ireland.

▲ **LAUNCHED:** May 31, 1911

▲ **LENGTH:** 882 feet. The ship was longer than the height of the world's tallest building in 1912.

▲ **WIDTH:** 92.5 feet

▲ **MAX SPEED :** 21 knots (24 mph)

▲ **MAX CAPACITY:** 3,511 passengers and crew

THE RMS *TITANIC*

Titanic set out on its very first voyage from Southampton, England, to New York, USA, on April 10, 1912. The journey should have taken 7 days, but the liner crashed into an iceberg just 4 days into its trip.

THE 20 LIFEBOATS ON BOARD COULD CARRY UP TO 59 PEOPLE EACH, WHICH WAS NOT NEARLY ENOUGH TO SAVE ALL PASSENGERS AND CREW

2 YEARS

The time it took to build *Titanic*— plus 10 months to outfit the interior.

COMPARTMENTS DESIGNED TO TRAP WATER AND STOP THE SHIP FROM SINKING QUICKLY OVERFLOWED, SPEEDING UP THE DISASTER

 Titanic was nicknamed the "Millionaire's Special" because of all the wealthy people on board.

2.8 MILES

The depth beneath the ocean where *Titanic's* wreck lies today.

2.7 HOURS

The time the ship took to sink in the Atlantic Ocean on April 15, 1912, after crashing into the iceberg.

FRIGHTENING FIGURES!

Out of the estimated **2,224** passengers and crew on board, around **710** survived and **1,514** were killed in the disaster.

MEN
20%—SURVIVED

WOMEN
25%—SURVIVED

CHILDREN
50%—SURVIVED

THE SHIP'S EIGHT-PIECE ORCHESTRA PLAYED AT THE TOP OF ONE OF THE GRAND FIRST-CLASS STAIRCASES AS THE SHIP WENT DOWN

TURKISH BATHS

32-FT. HEATED SWIMMING POOL FOR FIRST-CLASS PASSENGERS ONLY

GUGLIELMO MARCONI'S NEW WIRELESS DEVICE ON THE BRIDGE MEANT *TITANIC* COULD RADIO OTHER SHIPS FOR AID, WHICH HELPED TO SAVE OVER 700 LIVES

GYMNASIUM

^ ALLURE OF THE SEAS

IT'S A RECORD!

ALLURE OF THE SEAS

1,187 FEET LONG

The length of the longest passenger ship built. It has 21 swimming pools and hot tubs, over 20 restaurants, an ice rink, and several theaters.

THE ICEBERG RIPPED A 300-FOOT GASH IN THE SIDE OF THE SHIP

THE WATER TEMPERATURE WAS AROUND 28°F. NO ONE COULD SURVIVE IN IT FOR MORE THAN ABOUT 15 MINUTES.

STAGGERING POOLS

It's always been cool to have a pool. For thousands of years people have used them for religious ceremonies, socializing, sports, and exercise.

SAN ALFONSO DEL MAR
CHIL

MARINA BAY SANDS HOTEL, SINGAPORE

FACT FILE

POOL HISTORY

◢ 4,500 YEARS AGO
The Great Bath at Mohenjo-daro, Pakistan, was built. Made of brick, it is 39 feet long and was probably used for religious ceremonies rather than swim training.

◢ 2,400 YEARS AGO
School children had their first swimming lessons. Ancient Greeks thought swimming was just as important as math and astronomy.

◢ 2,100 YEARS AGO
Roman Emperor Gaius Maecenas built the first known heated swimming pool.

SHANG-HIGH!

Shanghai's Holiday Inn has a 98-ft. pool that's 24 floors up. It has a glass bottom, and the deep end hangs right out over the edge of the building—eek!

BLOOD RED

The color of a famous hotel pool on Koh Samui, Thailand. The water is actually totally clear; the color comes from the red, orange, and yellow tiles that line the pool.

Infinity pools look as though they go on forever, or plunge over an edge. Overflowing water is actually caught in a low-lying basin and pumped back into the pool.

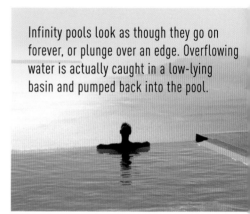

SAN ALFONSO DEL MAR

The world's largest saltwater swimming pool opened in Chile at San Alfonso del Mar Resort in 2006.

AT 3,323 FT. LONG, SWIMMING FROM END TO END WOULD BE LIKE SWIMMIMG 20 LENGTHS OF AN OLYMPIC POOL!

PACIFIC OCEAN

THIS POOL IS A WHOPPING 492 FT. LONG!

57 FLOORS UP, IT LOOKS OVER SINGAPORE'S FINANCIAL DISTRICT

MARINA BAY SANDS HOTEL

Marina Bay Sands Hotel in Singapore has the world's largest rooftop swimming pool in its Sky Park.

WATER SEEMS TO FLOW RIGHT OVER THE EDGE, BUT THERE'S AN UNSEEN RIDGE, SO SWIMMERS CAN'T FALL OFF

AT 115 FT. DEEP, THIS IS ALSO ONE OF THE DEEPEST MAN-MADE POOLS ON THE PLANET, WITH CRYSTAL-CLEAR WATER ALL THE WAY DOWN TO THE BOTTOM

VISITORS CAN SAIL BOATS, PADDLE CANOES, RIDE JET SKIS, AND EVEN SCUBA DIVE IN THESE CLEAR BLUE WATERS

HOW DEEP?

At up to 131 ft. deep and complete with underwater caves, Italy's Y40 is the world's deepest swimming pool for scuba diving. And because it's filled with warm, natural thermal water, you won't need a wetsuit.

MYSTERIOUS PYRAMIDS

Civilizations around the world have built pyramids, but the Great Pyramid at Giza, Egypt, is thought to be the largest of them all. It's the only one of the Seven Wonders of the Ancient World that is still standing today.

THE GREAT PYRAMID

For 3,800 years, the Great Pyramid held the record for the tallest structure in the world!

FACT FILE

◢ The Great Pyramid is the tomb of Pharaoh Khufu and was completed around 2551 BCE.

◢ Pharaoh Khufu's red granite coffin was placed in a small chamber in the very center of the pyramid.

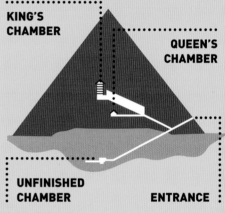

KING'S CHAMBER

QUEEN'S CHAMBER

UNFINISHED CHAMBER

ENTRANCE

GIZA, EGYPT

THE PYRAMID HAS SHRUNK IN HEIGHT, FROM 482 FT. TO 451 FT., BECAUSE MOST OF ITS OUTER CASING WAS STOLEN OR HAS WORN AWAY

2.3 MILLION STONE BLOCKS WERE USED TO BUILD THE PYRAMID; ACCORDING TO ONE CALCULATION, A BLOCK WAS LAID EVERY 2.5 MINUTES

WHEN THE PYRAMID WAS FIRST BUILT, IT WAS WHITE AND THE SIDES WERE STRAIGHT, WITH A SMOOTH LIMESTONE CASING

THE FOUR SIDES OF THE PYRAMID LINE UP WITH THE FOUR POINTS OF A COMPASS

EACH SIDE OF THE BASE SQUARE IS 755 FT. LONG

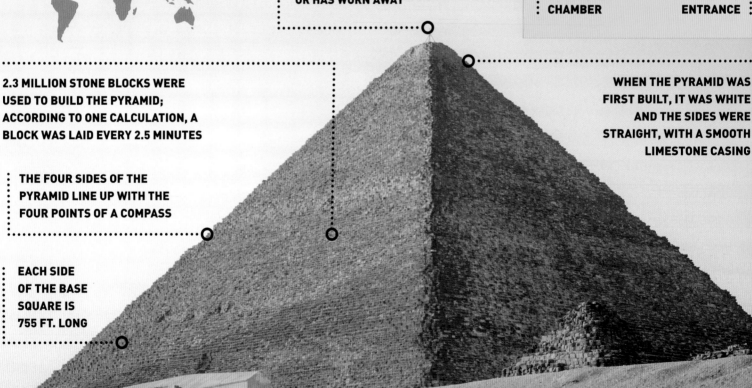

^ PYRAMID OF DJOSER, EGYPT

IT'S A RECORD!

OLDEST

The oldest existing Egyptian pyramid was built as a tomb for King Djoser (2630 BCE to 2611 BCE). It's 200 ft. tall and built on six huge levels that look like giant steps.

Stones were carried to the building site on rafts along the River Nile, then hoisted up earth ramps by heaving sleds over logs. The stones were then cut to shape and positioned so that each new layer was narrower than the last.

WONKY! PYRAMID

The Bent Pyramid (2565 BCE) suddenly changes its angle at the top. It's thought that workers started building the sides too steep and then decided to alter them!

^ MEROE PYRAMIDS, SUDAN

AROUND THE WORLD

◣ MESOPOTAMIA

Mesopotamia (now Iraq), had the world's first known pyramids, called ziggurats. These were step pyramids, and they date back at least 5,000 years!

◣ MEROE PYRAMIDS

One small section of desert in Sudan has nearly 200 pyramid tombs—more than in the whole of Egypt. "Meroe" pyramids are small, have steep walls, and some may be up to 2,700 years old.

◣ LATIN AMERICA

There are more pyramids in Latin America than in the whole of the rest of the world. These are typically step pyramids, with stairs up each side and a temple on the top.

20 YEARS
‹‹‹‹‹‹‹‹‹‹‹‹‹‹‹
THE TIME IT TOOK UP FOR
25,000
WORKERS TO BUILD THE GREAT PYRAMID

WHY A PYRAMID?

For big, tall buildings, this shape is incredibly sturdy and strong. It could also represent the rays of the sun, or a stairway to the afterlife.

A PERFECT PYRAMID HAS:

◣ Four vertical faces made from identical equilateral triangles *(whose sides are the same length)*

◣ A square base *(all four sides are the same length)*

^ TEOTIHUACAN, MEXICO

SPORTS SPECTACULAR

After a fire destroyed Rome's old wooden amphitheater, in 64 CE Emperor Vespasian decided to build the world's greatest entertainment venue. The ruins of the Colosseum still exist, but today many other stadiums are chasing its title.

ROME, ITAL

THE COLOSSEUM

Horrific games took place here. Animals were hunted in the arena, gladiators fought each other to the death, and men were killed by lions and bears.

IT TOOK 1,000 SAILORS TO INSTALL A HUGE SILK AWNING OVER THE TOP OF THE BUILDING TO PROTECT SPECTATORS FROM THE SUN

POOR PEOPLE SAT ON WOODEN BENCHES AT THE TOP—THEY HAD TO BRING THEIR OWN CUSHIONS

UP TO 28 ELEVATORS COULD LAUNCH ANIMALS, PEOPLE, AND PROPS THROUGH TRAP DOORS INTO THE ARENA FROM TUNNELS DOWN BELOW

THE 80 ARCHWAYS ON EACH OF THE FIRST THREE STORIES ALLOWED LIGHT INTO THE OUTER PASSAGEWAYS

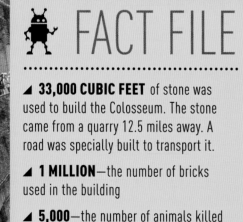

FACT FILE

◢ **33,000 CUBIC FEET** of stone was used to build the Colosseum. The stone came from a quarry 12.5 miles away. A road was specially built to transport it.

◢ **1 MILLION**—the number of bricks used in the building

◢ **5,000**—the number of animals killed in the Colosseum's first games

^ WATER CUBE, BEIJING

THE **WATER CUBE**

❮❮❮❮❮❮❮❮❮❮❮

The Water Cube was built for swimming events at the Beijing Olympics in 2008. It has a rectangular steel frame, but it's covered with a lightweight transparent film that's shaped to look like gigantic bubbles.

RED, WHITE, OR BLUE?

Lights under the transparent cladding of Munich's Allianz Arena change color, depending on which team is playing.

HE WOODEN ARENA FLOOR WAS
OVERED IN SAND TO SOAK UP
HE BLOOD, AND SOMETIMES THE
AND WAS MIXED WITH GLITTERY
OCK TO MAKE IT SPARKLE

SEATING SPACE FOR 50,000 SPECTATORS WITH LONG ROWS OF STONE STEPS ANGLED TO GIVE EVERYONE THE BEST POSSIBLE VIEW

IT'S A RECORD!

SHAKE THE ROOM

The echoey half-dome roof of CenturyLink Center in Seattle helped spark a mini earthquake, when fans won the record for the "loudest crowd roar in a sports stadium" in 2013.

SLIDING **FIELD**

Japan's Sapporo Dome is set up for baseball games. However, to host an indoor soccer match, a wall opens up, the seating is rearranged, and the outside field slides right into the stadium!

THE ARENA FLOOR
MEASURES 246 FT .
BY 144 FT.

 99,354
SPECTATORS

❯❯❯❯❯❯❯❯❯❯❯❯❯

The capacity of Barcelona's Camp Nou in Spain—Europe's largest football stadium since 1957.

SNOW BUSINESS

Snow and ice are fantastic building materials, but they do have one problem: they melt. Each year ice hotels trickle away in the spring, and just like igloos, they have to be built from scratch the following winter!

ICEHOTEL

Sweden's Icehotel, in Jukkasjärvi near the Arctic Circle, was the world's first ever ice hotel, and it's still the biggest.

JUKKASJÄRVI HOTEL, SWEDEN

 FACT FILE

◢ Specially designed ice saws cut 4,400 tons of pure ice from the frozen Torne River in spring. The blocks need to settle and are stored at a constant cool temperature over the summer.

◢ Building the hotel starts in November and takes six weeks.

◢ It takes 100 people to build the Icehotel, including 50 artists and designers who create works of ice art inside.

THE HOTEL STRUCTURES ARE BUILT AROUND METAL FRAMES. "SNICE" (SNOW AND ICE) IS FIRED OVER THE FRAMES

THE SNOW TAKES 2 DAYS TO SET, THEN THE METAL FRAMES ARE CAREFULLY REMOVED

THE LAYER OF SNICE IS SMOOTHED OVER BY HAND

THIS SHAPE IS KNOWN AS A CATENARY ARCH—IT'S REALLY STRONG, SO IT CAN SUPPORT ITS OWN WEIGHT

ICE BLOCKS ARE ROUGHENED AROUND THE EDGES AND THEN GLUED TOGETHER WITH WATER

"SNICE"

Snice is a special mixture of snow and ice, made by the builders. When it sets, it is as solid as cement.

The amount of snice used to build an ice hotel is enough to make

30,000

snowmen!

23°F

The coldest temperature inside an ice hotel

14°F *to* 23°F

The perfect conditions for building with ice and snow

–40°F

The coldest temperature outside an ice hotel— ***brrr!***

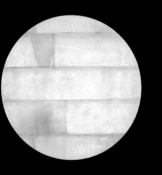

IGLOO = a traditional, temporary home built by Inuit people hunting in northern Canada and Greenland.

IGLOO FACTS

30—the number of people the largest Inuit igloos could accommodate

1 HOUR—the time it takes to build a small igloo (if you know what you're doing!)

2 FT. x 4 FT.—the size of an average igloo brick

SUPER STRONG

Warmth inside an igloo melts the snow on the outside. As the meltwater refreezes and sets, it strengthens the structure.

(ABOVE)
AN ICE SCULPTURE CREATED AT THE HARBIN FESTIVAL IN HEILONGJIANG, CHINA

COLOSSAL CASTLES

Castles are some of history's biggest and strongest structures. Designed to protect the important people who lived inside them from attack, they had to be built to last.

> KRAK DES CHEVALIERS, SYRIA

FACT FILE

◢ Krak des Chevaliers (right) was built during the Crusades (wars between Christians and Muslims) by knights called Hospitallers—Christian warrior monks. They occupied the castle from 1142 to 1271.

◢ It's known as a concentric castle because it has two sets of walls with a moat in between them.

◢ After an earthquake destroyed most of the castle in 1170, the Hospitallers rebuilt it, making it bigger and stronger.

◢ Just looking at the castle was enough to deter enemies from trying to attack.

2,000 x
1,000 x

Krak des Chevaliers could accommodate a garrison of 2,000 soldiers, and its stables could hold 1,000 horses.

KRAK DES CHEVALIERS

This castle was so strong that it was never successfully taken by force.

THE INNER WALLS ARE BUILT INTO THE ROCK BENEATH, WHICH MAKES THEM EARTHQUAKE-PROOF, AND THE SMOOTH, SLOPING LIMESTONE MEANT CLIMBING THESE WALLS WAS IMPOSSIBLE

THE POSITION, 2,132 FT. ABOVE SEA LEVEL, WAS IDEAL FOR GUARDING THE PASS BELOW THAT LED TO THE MEDITERRANEAN

OUTER WALLS ARE LOWER, SO THE KNIGHTS COULD ALWAYS STAY ABOVE THEIR ATTACKERS

10 FT. THICK WALLS

7 YEARS

How long a siege of Harlech Castle, Wales, lasted in the fifteenth century. It was the longest siege in British history.

IT'S A RECORD!

HOW LONG?

Burghausen Castle in Germany dates back to 1255. With walls measuring over 3,448 ft., it's the longest castle in the world.

CASTLE VOCAB

SIEGE—an attack that involved surrounding a castle, trapping people inside, and cutting off its supplies

TALUS—sloping castle wall

LOOPHOLE—a window just wide enough to fire an arrow through

NNER BUILDINGS INCLUDED A ANQUET HALL, A CHAPEL, KITCHENS, ND A 394 FT.-LONG STORAGE ROOM HAT HELD ENOUGH SUPPLIES TO LAST FIVE-YEAR SIEGE!

OUND TOWERS HELP TO TRENGTHEN THE WALLS, ND THE STONES WERE AND-CARVED INTO SHAPE

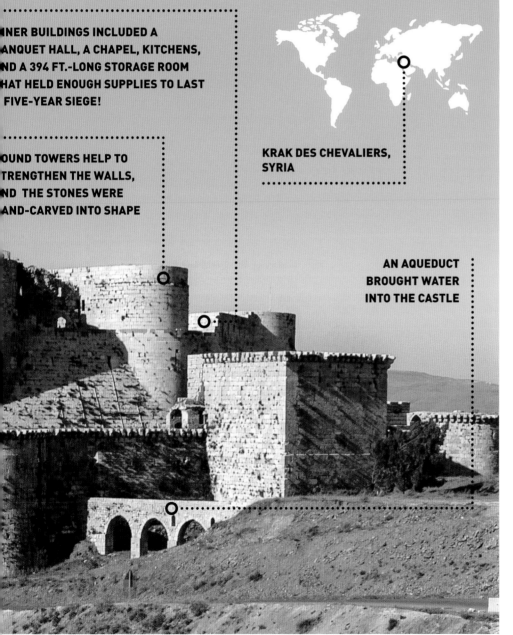

KRAK DES CHEVALIERS, SYRIA

AN AQUEDUCT BROUGHT WATER INTO THE CASTLE

600

The number of castles in Wales—more than any other country in Europe. It includes Iron Age, Roman, and Medieval fortresses.

^ PREDJAMA CASTLE, SLOVENIA

CASTLE IN A CAVE

Predjama Castle, Slovenia, (above) is built into a cave, 403.5 ft. up in the cliffs. The building itself is 115 ft. tall and over 700 years old.

IMPOSSIBLE RAILWAYS

It took a huge workforce to build the first railways in the eighteenth and early nineteenth century. But constructing everything by hand didn't stop engineers and governments from planning some unbelievable routes.

THE MOST DIFFICULT RAILWAY IN THE WORLD

That's the nickname for the Nariz del Diablo (Devil's Nose) railway track, which runs through the Andes in Ecuador. It's a spectacular trip, passing the world's largest active volcano, the mountain peak that's closest to the sun, the "Avenue of Volcanoes," and riding over the top of Devil's Nose rock.

NARIZ DEL DIABLO RAILWAY, EQUADOR

FACT FILE

◢ The route runs from Ecuador's capital, Quito, to the main port of Guayaquil.

◢ **288 MILES** The length of the route

◢ **25–30 DAYS** How long it took to transport goods from port to city before the railway came

◢ **4 DAYS AND 3 NIGHTS** The time the journey takes by tourist train today

◢ The project was riddled with problems, from floods, landslides, and earthquakes to revolutions, assassinations, terrorist attacks, and bankruptcy . . . not to mention bubonic plague!

INSTEAD OF GOING AROUND THE ROCK, THE TRACK ZIGZAGS RIGHT OVER THE TOP

DEVIL'S NOSE IS A HUGE WALL OF ROCK THAT REALLY DOES LOOK LIKE A GIANT NOSE

FOR THE MOST SPECTACULAR VIEWS, PASSENGERS USED TO TRAVEL ON THE ROOF OF THE TRAIN!

37 YEARS

The time it took to build the Nariz del Diablo railway (including the hold-ups). It opened with a huge party in 1908.

The Nariz del Diablo railway climbs from 5,905 ft. to 8,530 ft.

2,625 FEET

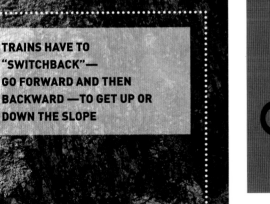

UNBELIEVABLE!

That's what engineers said about building a railway through the jungle between Rangoon in Burma and Bangkok in Thailand. The Japanese Army used a third of a million locals and prisoners of war (POWs) to build the railway during World War II.

5 YEARS
How long the British estimated it would take to build

1.5 YEARS
The time the Japanese actually took to complete it

120,000
The number of workers under the Japanese army who died on the job

LIZARD LUNCH

The POWs who built the Burma Railway were treated as slaves. They survived on weevil-infested rice, as well as lizards and snakes they caught in the jungle.

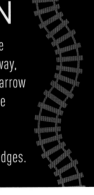

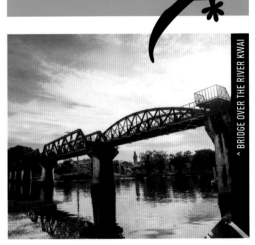

^ BRIDGE OVER THE RIVER KWAI

TRAINS HAVE TO "SWITCHBACK"— GO FORWARD AND THEN BACKWARD —TO GET UP OR DOWN THE SLOPE

1825
The world's first public railway line opened to carry coal from Stockton to Darlington, UK.

TOY TRAIN

That's the nickname for the Darjeeling Himalayan Railway, with its small trains and narrow tracks. In just 55 miles, the mountain train climbs to 7,407 ft., turns around 873 bends, and crosses 554 bridges.

22,000 MILES
The amount of working rail track in Britain by 1900.

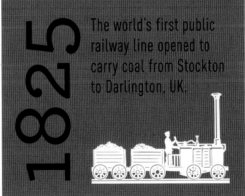

IT'S A RECORD!

155,350 MILES

The USA has the world's longest railway network, with 155,350 miles of track. A further 16,777 miles is due to open by 2030.

SUPER COLLIDER

The European particle physics laboratory CERN, near Geneva in Switzerland, is home to the Large Hadron Collider (LHC for short). The Collider isn't just large—it's huge! Scientists are using it to try to find answers to questions about the past and future of our universe.

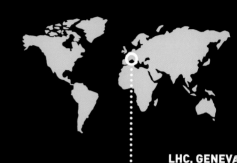

LHC, GENEVA SWITZERLAND

FACT FILE

▲ A particle accelerator is a machine that beams proton particles at fantastic speeds and causes them to smash into each other to create new particles.

▲ The LHC is buried underground beneath the borders of Switzerland and France.

▲ The main part of the LHC is this circular tunnel that's buried **328 ft.** underground.

▲ It has a circumference of **17 miles.**

WHAT A PICTURE!

At four points along the tunnel there are huge concrete caverns, each housing a "detector" that's a bit like an enormous digital camera. The detectors record the collisions the particles make so that physicists can analyze them and identify the particles.

49 FT. WIDE AND
49 FT. HIGH

THE LHC WAS BUILT IN 15 SECTIONS AND THEN LOWERED TO ITS UNDERGROUND HOME

WEIGHING 15,432 TONS, THE LHC IS BUILT OF TWICE AS MUCH IRON AS THE EIFFEL TOWER IN PARIS!

THE DETECTORS ARE MADE UP OF THOUSANDS OF SMALL, COMPLICATED PARTS AND HAVE TO BE CAREFULLY MAINTAINED

THE HUGE MAGNET IN ITS CORE HAS A MAGNETIC FIELD AT LEAST 100,000 TIMES STRONGER THAN THE EARTH'S

JLG LIFTLUX 153-12

IT'S A RECORD!

The LHC became the largest scientific instrument in the world when it was completed in 2008. It's also the world's most powerful particle accelerator.

10,000

The number of scientists and engineers connected with the project.

100

The number of countries that have been involved in the building and research.

−456.25 °F

The temperature inside the LHC.

10 YEARS

The time it took to build CERN.

Higgs boson

In 2012, scientists at LHC were able to prove that the "Higgs boson" really exists. The Higgs boson helps other particles to join together to form objects—like stars and planets.

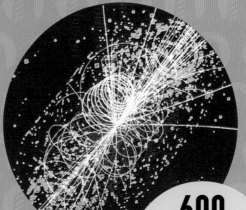

SMALL BEGINNINGS

The first particle accelerator was invented in 1930. It was less than 14 in. wide.

BIG BANG *THEORY*

Scientists at CERN use particle acceleration to recreate the effect of the Big Bang.

That's a theory of how the universe expanded from something very tiny into the universe we know today.

600 MILLION

The number of particle collisions the LHC can generate in one second.

AWESOME WATERWAYS

The idea to cut a watery passageway through Central America was first suggested in the sixteenth century. Work eventually started in 1881, but the waterway—the Panama Canal— became the most difficult engineering project in history.

PANAMA CANAL

PANAMA CANAL

1,700 ports and 160 countries are connected through the Panama Canal— it's become one of the world's most important waterways.

BOATS ARE LIFTED 85 FT. IN A SERIES OF LOCKS ON ONE SIDE, THEN LOWERED AGAIN TO SEA LEVEL ON THE OTHER SIDE

THE BIG DITCH that's the canal's nickname.

LOCK GATES UP TO 82 FT. TALL ARE OPERATED FROM A CONTROL TOWER

CONTAINER SHIPS CARRY UP TO 18,000 20-FT. CONTAINERS

PILOT BOATS ESCORT THE SHIPS ALONG THE CANAL

LARGER SHIPS ARE GUIDED THROUGH THE LOCK BY MECHANICAL "MULES"

FACT FILE

▲ Work on the canal hit many setbacks, before the canal officially opened in 1914.

▲ At times, more than 40,000 men from around 50 countries worked on the project, 6 days a week and for 10 hours a day!

▲ More than 25,000 workers died.

▲ Gatun Lake, which lies between the canal locks, was the largest man-made lake in history when it was completed in 1913.

▲ A massive new canal extension opened in 2016 provides wider entrances to the canal, deeper channels, and bigger locks.

▲ The canal cost a total of $639 million to build.

48 MILES

The length of the passage between the Atlantic and Pacific Oceans.

ATLANTIC OCEAN

— PANAMA CANAL

PACIFIC OCEAN

8–10 HOURS

The time it takes to cross today.

22 DAYS

The time it would take to travel around South America without using the canal.

8,000 miles

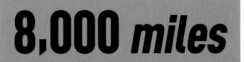

Thanks to the canal, the journey by boat from New York to California is 8,000 miles shorter than before.

^ GATUN LAKE, PANAMA CANAL

TRAFFIC JAM

13,000 ships use the canal each year; they sometimes queue for days to get in.

$1.8 BILLION

The total toll money ships pay each year.

HOW A LOCK WORKS

1. A ship enters the huge lock tank on one water level.

OPEN   CLOSED

2. Gates close behind it.

3. The lock fills with water and the ship rises up.

CLOSED   CLOSED

4. Gates open in front of it, and the ship sails through on a higher water level.

CLOSED   OPEN

KILLER MOSQUITOES

The main cause of worker deaths was insect-borne disease. Eventually "mosquito brigades" were set up to mosquito-proof the home and workplace.

^ BUILDING THE PANAMA CANAL

CARNIVAL GIANTS

Floats were first used in the Middle Ages to move scenery for religious plays. Today fantastic floats are created for parades around the world, but they don't last long.

Float—a vehicle carrying a display in a street parade.

ZUNDER NETHERLAND

RIO DE JANEIRO, BRAZIL

FACT FILE

◢ **20** The number of flower-decked floats that ride through Zundert, Netherlands, on the first Sunday in September.

◢ **3–4 MONTHS** The time it takes to build the float frames.

◢ **3 DAYS** The time, just before the parade, when the flowers are added (so they don't start to wilt).

◢ **2 DAYS** That's how long the floats are on display before being destroyed!

◢ Hidden under a tent, the floats are built inside a huge scaffold. Once the chassis is in place, the iron frame is welded together, then covered in papier mâché, before the flowers are attached.

The year of the first Zundert parade. It featured simple, dahlia-festooned bicycles and horse-drawn carts.

FLOWER POWER

Zundert Flower Parade is the largest flower parade in the world. It celebrates the region's production of dahlia flowers.

INCLUDING THE BIRD'S BEA WHICH OPENS AND CLOSE THERE ARE 53 MOVING PART

THIS FLOAT, CALLED "CRAZY GOLD," WON FIRST PLACE IN 2013

UP TO 400,000 DAHLIAS ARE NAILED ON TO EACH FLOAT BY HAND

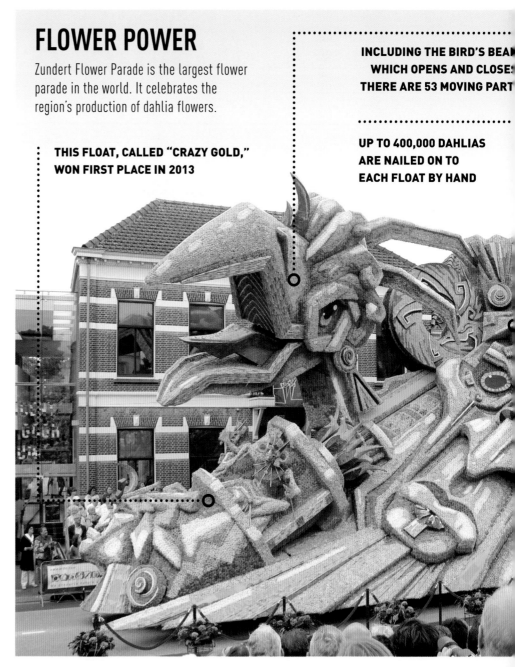

OVER 175 YEARS

How long floats have paraded in the New Orleans Mardi Gras. The first ones were carts drawn by mules.

THE FACE BELONGS TO AN AZTEC KING WHO WAS SO CRAZY ABOUT GOLD THAT HE HAD HIMSELF COVERED IN THE STUFF, AND IT WAS SAID THAT ANYONE WHO LOOKED AT HIM WOULD GO MAD!

^ THE SAMBODROMO, RIO DE JANEIRO

RIO CARNIVAL

The Rio Carnival in Brazil has become so big that instead of parading through the streets, the samba procession now has its own stadium—the Sambadrome—which is nearly half a mile long!

◢ Spectacular displays on the floats hide complex structures and mechanisms of glass, wood, iron, and steel. Each float has a theme and tells a story.

◢ The floats have to measure between 131–196 ft.

◢ The maximum width is 26–33 ft.

◢ Each Rio Carnival float can cost up to $250,000 to build.

IT'S A RECORD!

HOW LONG?

A pre-carnival party in Tesesina, Brazil, made a world record in 2012 for the longest parade, with 343 floats and a 6.5 hour parade.

MEGA CRANES

Cranes make the job of lifting and loading heavy weights much easier for humans. And as buildings, ships, and oil rigs get bigger, so do the cranes that construct, move, and unload them.

SHANGHAI, CHINA

WORKING IN THE SKY

The Shanghai World Financial Center is nearly 1,614 feet tall and has 101 stories. The cranes used to build it (right) had to climb up the walls as the structure grew!

FACT FILE

THE CRANE OPERATOR SITS HERE AND CAN'T BE SCARED OF HEIGHTS!

THE LIFTING CABLE IS AS LONG AS TEN JUMBO JETS AND CAN LIFT WEIGHTS OF 32 TONS AT A SPEED OF 118 FT. PER MINUTE

HOW A TOWER CRANE WORKS

Cranes operate with a system of pulleys. To lift a weight on one end of a cable, an equal lifting force needs to be applied at the other end.

COUNTERWEIGHT STOPS CRANE TOPPLING

JIB

CLIMBING CRANES RISE UP THE BUILDING WITH THE HELP OF HYDRAULIC ARMS AND ARE SUPPORTED BY STEEL BEAMS ATTACHED TO THE WALLS

CRANE WEIGHS 250 TONS

TROLLEY AND HOOK

CRANE OPERATOR

CRANE RISES WITH THE BUILDING

CONCRETE BASE ANCHORS THE CRANE

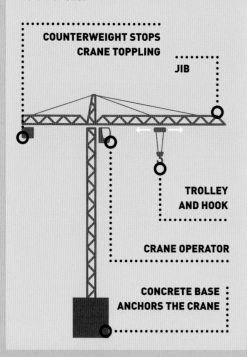

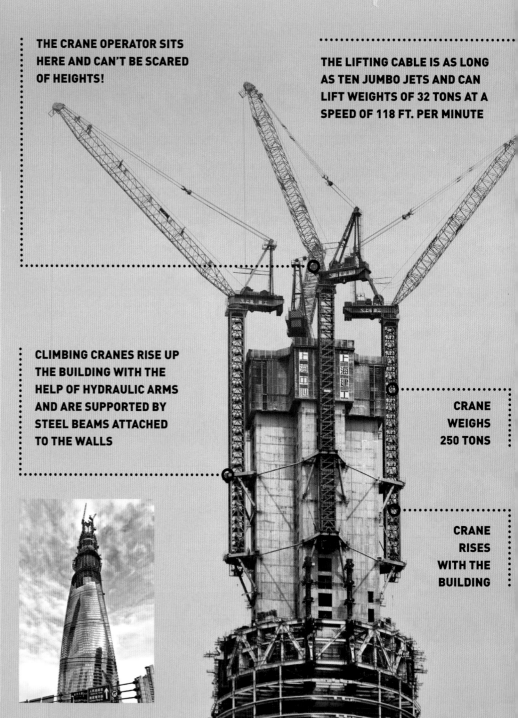

CRANE *TYPES*

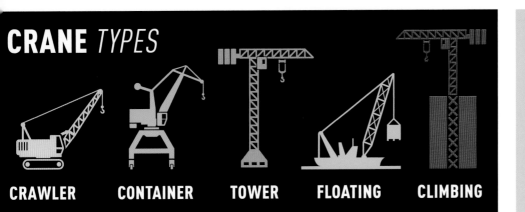

CRAWLER   **CONTAINER**   **TOWER**   **FLOATING**   **CLIMBING**

144 ft. PER MINUTE

The speed the cranes working on the Kingdom Tower—the world's next tallest building—can lift a load weighing 18 tons.

FIFTH CENTURY BCE

When ancient Greeks began using the first cranes with a single pulley.

<<<<<<<<<<<<<

FOURTH CENTURY BCE

When the compound pulley was developed. It's still being used today.

50

The number of men needed to move a 2.75-ton stone block in Egyptian times, 2–3,000 years ago, according to one theory.

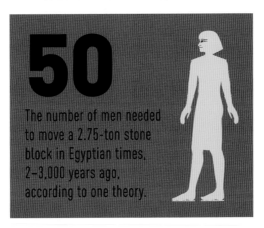

^ CONTAINER CRANE

^ THE DUTCH THIALF

IT'S A RECORD!

LARGEST

The world's largest floating crane is the Dutch Thialf, a floating barge that can lift 15,652 tons. It also has a helipad and can accommodate 736 people.

30 STORIES HIGH *(289 FT.)*

The size of some of the cranes used to load and unload the new, wider, supersized ships that operate on the Panama Canal.

CRANE CRASH!

In 2015, a huge crawler crane snapped in half during a violent rainstorm in Mecca, Saudi Arabia, killing more than 100 people and injuring many more. It was the deadliest crane accident in history.

I Lift NY

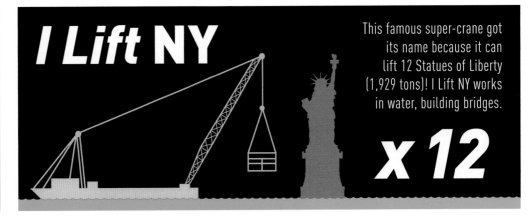

This famous super-crane got its name because it can lift 12 Statues of Liberty (1,929 tons)! I Lift NY works in water, building bridges.

x 12

KEEP IT GREEN

The idea of growing plants away from their natural habitat has been around since Roman times. Today it's even possible to cultivate an indoor rainforest in England!

THE EDEN PROJECT

In 1995, the Eden Project in Cornwall, UK, was a barren old clay pit. Today it's a gigantic garden, housing two greenhouse domes. The bigger dome is the world's largest greenhouse, and inside is the largest enclosed jungle in the world.

THE BUBBLE EFFECT—CREATED WITH HEXAGON- AND PENTAGON-SHAPED FRAMES—FITS IN WITH THE UNEVEN SURFACE OF THE LANDSCAPE

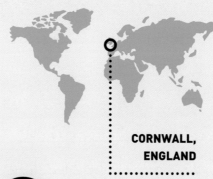

CORNWALL, ENGLAND

The domes are south-facing, to catch the sun.

FACT FILE

▲ The design of the Eden Project domes was inspired by soap bubbles because they can land on any surface.

▲ The steel tubes that make the frames only weigh a little more than the air inside the domes.

▲ Concrete "anchors" ensure the super-light domes don't blow away.

▲ The windows weigh just 1 percent of the equivalent amount of glass, but they are strong enough to take the weight of a car!

STRAIGHT LINES JOIN THE DOMES IN THE SAME WAY SOAP BUBBLES JOIN TOGETHER

THE WINDOWS ARE MADE FROM A TRIPLE LAYER OF SUPER-STRONG MATERIAL RATHER LIKE CLING FILM; THEY LET IN LIGHT AND KEEP IN WARMTH

EACH HEXAGON FRAME MEASURES UP 36 FT. ACRO

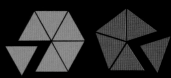

SKY MONKEYS

The Eden Project nickname for the abseilers who fitted the windows and the rope-trained gardeners who look after the plants 160 ft. up.

1,185 PLANTS

grow inside the Rainforest Biome, including banana trees, rubber trees, and giant bamboo. There's even a waterfall!

PUMP IT UP!

Each hexagonal window is like a pillow pumped up with air. On a cold day, pumping in more air warms up the biome. On warm days, letting air out cools it down.

RADICAL RECYCLING AT EDEN:

▲ Rainwater provides 43 percent of the water supply, thanks to an underground drainage pit.

▲ Old truck tires provide mats.

▲ Beer bottles provide glass tiles.

▲ Maize provides carpets.

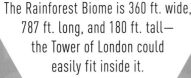

The Rainforest Biome is 360 ft. wide, 787 ft. long, and 180 ft. tall—the Tower of London could easily fit inside it.

Geodesic biodome in Montreal, Canada

THE FIRST GREENHOUSE

In 30 CE, Emperor Tiberius ate cucumbers grown in a "specularium." Its walls were made of stone, and outside fires kept the cucumbers warm. A special stone lid allowed light in.

ECO-SPEAK

BIOME—a group of plants and other living things occupying a specific habitat—for example, a rainforest.

HEXAGON—a six-sided shape. Hexagons make up honeycombs and work well in architecture because the sides fit together without leaving a gap.

GEODESIC DOMES are built with a framework of connecting shapes such as triangles, pentagons (shapes with five sides), or hexagons.

SPACE STATION

Thousands of man-made satellites orbit the Earth—it's often possible to spot some of them in a clear night sky. You might be able to see the International Space Station speeding on its way, too.

ISS

The International Space Station (ISS for short) is a laboratory, a living space for six people, and the largest satellite in the sky.

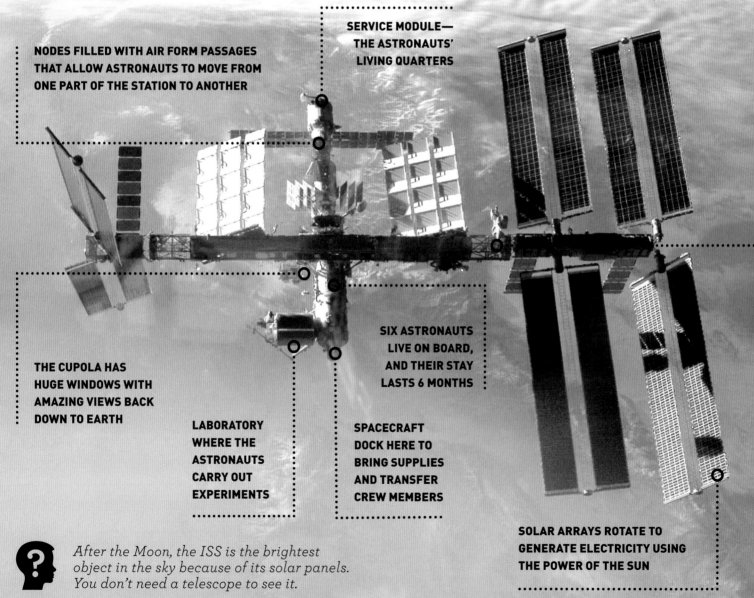

THE ISS ORBITS, ON AVERAGE, 220 MILES ABOVE THE EARTH

THE DIFFERENT MODULES ARE ATTACHED TO A CENTRAL SECTION, CALLED THE TRUSS

SERVICE MODULE— THE ASTRONAUTS' LIVING QUARTERS

NODES FILLED WITH AIR FORM PASSAGES THAT ALLOW ASTRONAUTS TO MOVE FROM ONE PART OF THE STATION TO ANOTHER

THE CUPOLA HAS HUGE WINDOWS WITH AMAZING VIEWS BACK DOWN TO EARTH

SIX ASTRONAUTS LIVE ON BOARD, AND THEIR STAY LASTS 6 MONTHS

LABORATORY WHERE THE ASTRONAUTS CARRY OUT EXPERIMENTS

SPACECRAFT DOCK HERE TO BRING SUPPLIES AND TRANSFER CREW MEMBERS

SOLAR ARRAYS ROTATE TO GENERATE ELECTRICITY USING THE POWER OF THE SUN

After the Moon, the ISS is the brightest object in the sky because of its solar panels. You don't need a telescope to see it.

FACT FILE

◢ The ISS is designed to observe the Earth, study space, and act as a refueling stop for spaceships. Research into microgravity on the ISS might help future missions to reach unexplored planets.

◢ Construction of the ISS started in 1998. Because of its weight, the station was constructed in space.

◢ The first crew moved in in 2000, and the ISS has been manned ever since.

◢ The living space inside the ISS is about the size of a five-bedroom house, but without the comforts of home.There are no chairs or beds—weightlessness means astronauts never need to sit down!

5 MILES *PER SEC*

That's how fast the station travels. It orbits Earth every 90 minutes—the distance covered is equivalent to traveling from Earth to the Moon and back every day.

Over 200 people from 15 different countries have stayed on the ISS. Sleeping compartments are cupboard-sized, with a sleeping bag inside. Being weightless, the crew can sleep upside down if they like!

ZZZZ

Space Wheat

Russia's Mir Space Station was launched in 1986 and was the first to be assembled in orbit. It was designed to last five years, but went on for 15. Mir astronauts even grew the first crop of wheat from seeds in space!

SPACE STATIONS TIMELINE

1940s > The idea for a space station was formed, with plans drawn up in the 1950s.

1960s > Unmanned spacecraft explored and photographed the Moon. In 1969, two Russian space vehicles linked to form the first space station.

1970s > Skylab, the first US space station, proved humans could survive in space for long periods.

1980s > The reusable space shuttle made the idea of building structures in space more realistic.

It took **40 MISSIONS** to transport around **100 PARTS** to build the ISS, and **160 SPACEWALKS** to connect and maintain them.

^ THE SPACE SHUTTLE DOCKING WITH ISS

When ISS astronauts need something they don't have, they can print it using a 3-D printer. Many objects have been printed in space, including tools, such as a ratchet and a wrench.

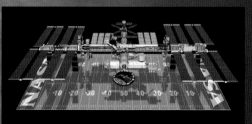

THE **ISS** IS ROUGHLY THE SIZE OF AN **NFL FOOTBALL FIELD.**

IT'S A RECORD!

$100 BILLION

The estimated cost of constructing ISS. It's the most expensive object ever built and the largest ever built in space.

STRANGE-SHAPED STRUCTURES

Sometimes shapes are just for fun; sometimes they have a purpose, but today it's possible to create a structure that looks like just about anything you can imagine!

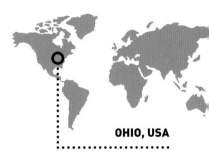

OHIO, USA

THE BASKET BUILDING

This strange-looking building in Ohio, USA, is the headquarters of a company called Longaberger, and it was designed to look like one of the company's own products.

84 WINDOWS

THE BASKET HANDLES ARE HEATED SO THAT THEY DON'T ICE OVER

THE BUILDING IS 160 TIMES LARGER THAN THE BASKET IT MIMICS

THE TAG IS PAINTED WITH GOLD LEAF AND WEIGHS 725 LB.

THE WOVEN EFFECT IS MADE WITH A TYPE OF SYNTHETIC PLASTER

IT'S A RECORD!

BIGGEST ELEPHANT

The 32-floor Elephant Tower in Bangkok is the world's largest elephant-shaped building!

A Moving Building

Prague's Dancing House is also called "Fred and Ginger" because it's supposed to look like the famous dancing duo. Fred is made from concrete with a wire sculpture for hair; Ginger has a glass dress and concrete dancing legs.

$50,000 A DAY

The cost of renting South Korea's Mr. Toilet House. The building was designed to mark a meeting of the World Toilet Association. It's made of white concrete, steel, and glass, and it even has a hole in the middle!

EARS ARE BALCONIES
EYES ARE HUGE WINDOWS
TUSKS ARE OFFICES

^ THE ELEPHANT TOWER

 FACT FILE

THE GHERKIN TOWER gets its nickname because of its similarity to a pickle, but its cylindrical shape has many advantages:

◢ The shape is very strong, so it doesn't need supporting columns.

◢ The tower's curves allow more space for other tall buildings around it.

◢ The bulge in the middle lessens the chance of strong winds at the base.

◢ The triangular windows add strength to the building.

◢ The shape allows lots of sunlight to enter the building.

^ THE GHERKIN TOWER

LEANING TOWERS

Everyone's heard of Italy's Leaning Tower of Pisa, but it isn't the only leaning tower in the world—and it isn't the oldest either. Some modern structures have even been designed to lean.

PISA'S LEANING TOWER

PISA, ITALY

HEIGHT: 186 FT.

THE SEVEN BELLS IN THE BELL CHAMBER STOPPED RINGING IN THE TWENTIETH CENTURY—THE SOUND COULD HAVE CAUSED THE TOWER TILT EVEN FARTHER

HEIGHT: 183 FT.

THE ARCHITECT TRIED TO CORRECT THE LEAN BY BUILDING THE UPPER FLOORS TALLER ON THE SHORTER SIDE, BUT THE ATTEMPT FAILED

FACT FILE

▲ Work on the white marble Tower of Pisa began in 1173. It was already leaning by the time the third floor was finished in 1178.

▲ Work stopped for a war and to solve the tower's problems. The building was left for 100 years, allowing the soil time to compress. This kept it from collapsing.

▲ For 800 years, the tower fell by 0.078 in. per year. In the 1920s, cement was pumped into the foundations to help halt the shift.

▲ The tower leaned by 5.5 degrees in the 1990s, but removing soil and stabilizing the foundations reduced the lean to under 4 degrees.

WORK STOPPED HERE IN 1178

THE CLAY SOIL WASN'T FIRM ENOUGH TO HOLD THE 16,000-TON BUILDING

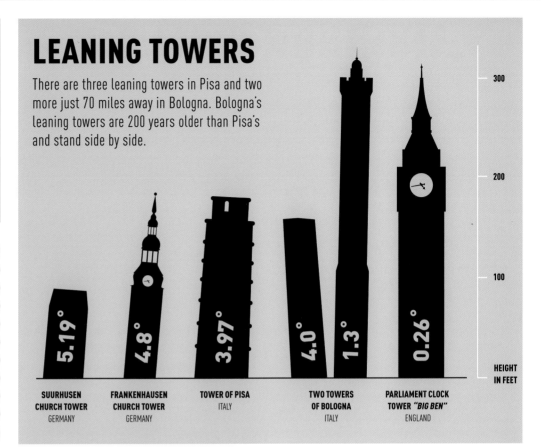

^ SUURHUSEN, GERMANY

LEANING TOWERS

There are three leaning towers in Pisa and two more just 70 miles away in Bologna. Bologna's leaning towers are 200 years older than Pisa's and stand side by side.

300
200
100
HEIGHT IN FEET

5.19°	4.8°	3.97°	4.0°	1.3°	0.26°
SUURHUSEN CHURCH TOWER GERMANY	FRANKENHAUSEN CHURCH TOWER GERMANY	TOWER OF PISA ITALY	TWO TOWERS OF BOLOGNA ITALY		PARLIAMENT CLOCK TOWER "BIG BEN" ENGLAND

IT'S A RECORD!

5.19° LEAN

A thirteenth-century church tower in Suurhusen, Germany, is officially the world's "farthest leaning tower." Built on marshy ground, its rotting wooden supports are causing the tilt.

TWISTED TOWER

Chesterfield's thirteeth-century church spire has shrunk on one side and now leans by 9 ft. 5 in. One theory about its lean is that the tower was wrongly constructed with green timber because all the skilled workers had been killed off by the Black Death!

4,000 YEARS

How long it would take the Big Ben clock tower to tilt as far as the Tower of Pisa. Big Ben's tower is leaning at an angle of 0.26° because of underground sewers, Tube tunnels, and car parks.

Cool Curve

The world title of "farthest man-made leaning tower" belongs to Capital Gate in Abu Dhabi, which tilts a whopping 18°. The building rises straight to the 12th story, where the curve begins, and it straightens again toward the top.

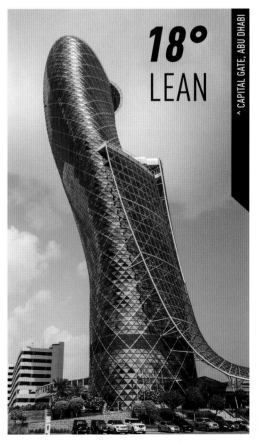

^ CAPITAL GATE, ABU DHABI

18° LEAN

ART-ITECTURE

When it comes to building for the arts, architects are often expected to come up with something new—a building that looks like a work of art itself.

THE SYDNEY OPERA HOUSE

Eight Boeing 747 airplanes could fit side by side on the site of the Sydney Opera House.

SYDNEY, AUSTRALIA

Jutting out into the sea, the Opera House has been called a masterpiece of creativity. It's listed as a UNESCO World Heritage Site.

THE GLASS WAS MADE TO ORDER AND CAME ALL THE WAY FROM FRANCE

OVER 1 MILLION SPECIALLY-MADE ROOF TILES REFLECT THE SUN AND DON'T SHOW DIRT

THE PEAK IS THE HEIGHT OF A 20-STORY BUILDING

THE ROOF IS CONSTRUCTED FROM 2,194 CONCRETE PIECES WEIGHING UP TO 15 TONS EACH, AND SPECIAL CRANES WERE BUILT TO FIT THEM

PANELS MADE OF GRANITE

THE SHAPE OF THE ROOF SAILS IS DESIGNED TO SUIT THE WATERSIDE LOCATION

FACT FILE

▲ Architect Jørn Utzon wanted the building to look like a sculpture, reflecting its Sydney Harbour location.

▲ 10,000 builders were employed on the site when work started in 1959. The Opera House wasn't completed until 1973.

▲ It took eight years to design and figure out a way to build the roof sails.

▲ Inside, the Opera House has 1,000 rooms and hosts 3,000 events each year.

▲ The building has 2 main performance spaces—one for opera and one for symphony concerts. The Concert Hall seats 2,679 spectators.

Inside Out

The Centre Georges Pompidou (right) was designed for people who don't normally like galleries. To make the most of the inside space, the steel frame of the building and its utility pipes are visible on the outside. These are color-coded and help to turn the building into a fun work of modern art.

Beijing's National Center for the Performing Arts (below) looks like an egg when the building is reflected in water! There's no sign of an entrance into the structure; instead, visitors enter through a tunnel that runs underneath the lake.

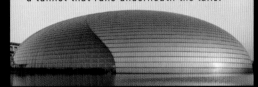

^ POMPIDOU CENTER, PARIS

IT'S A RECORD!

3,800 👤👤

New York's Metropolitan Opera House seats 3,800 people—more than any other opera house in the world.

^ WALT DISNEY CONCERT HALL, LOS ANGELES

JET SET

Contractors were baffled by the sculptural designs for the Walt Disney Concert Hall (above) in Los Angeles, USA. Help came in the form of 3-D interactive computer software that's normally used to design fighter jets.

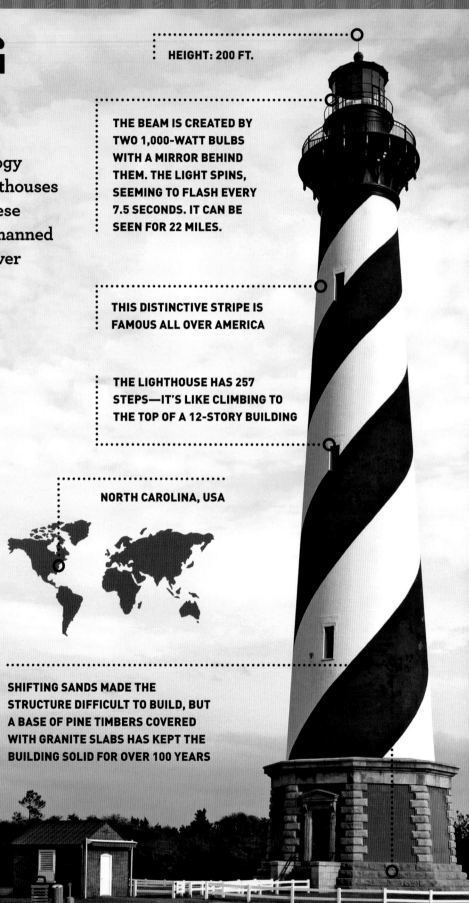

BEAMING BUILDINGS

New techniques and modern technology mean seafarers no longer rely on lighthouses as much as they used to. However, these beaming towers and the people who manned them have saved thousands of lives over the centuries.

CAPE HATTERAS LIGHTHOUSE

Two currents meet at Diamond Shoals, off the coast of North Carolina, USA, creating sandbanks, which are deadly to ships that stray off course.

 FACT FILE

◢ Around 800 BCE, flaming beacons were lit on hilltops to guide ships at sea.

◢ The remains of a Roman lighthouse dated 41–54 CE still stands in Dover, UK. It was once 79 ft. tall.

◢ In 1326, the Genoa lighthouse started using olive oil lamps. In 1543, at 253 ft. tall and 389 ft. above sea level, the new Genoa lighthouse became the tallest in the Mediterranean.

◢ The USA once had 3,000 lighthouses; now only 600 are left.

◢ Today most lighthouses are automatic, and ships have their own navigation equipment. Lighted buoys sometimes warn of danger.

HEIGHT: 200 FT.

THE BEAM IS CREATED BY TWO 1,000-WATT BULBS WITH A MIRROR BEHIND THEM. THE LIGHT SPINS, SEEMING TO FLASH EVERY 7.5 SECONDS. IT CAN BE SEEN FOR 22 MILES.

THIS DISTINCTIVE STRIPE IS FAMOUS ALL OVER AMERICA

THE LIGHTHOUSE HAS 257 STEPS—IT'S LIKE CLIMBING TO THE TOP OF A 12-STORY BUILDING

NORTH CAROLINA, USA

SHIFTING SANDS MADE THE STRUCTURE DIFFICULT TO BUILD, BUT A BASE OF PINE TIMBERS COVERED WITH GRANITE SLABS HAS KEPT THE BUILDING SOLID FOR OVER 100 YEARS

WHAT A WASHOUT

The first offshore lighthouse was completed on England's Eddystone Reef in 1699. The wooden building, lit by 60 candles, prevented shipwrecks for four years. But during the Great Storm of 1703, the building, along with its creator, Henry Winstanley, was washed away.

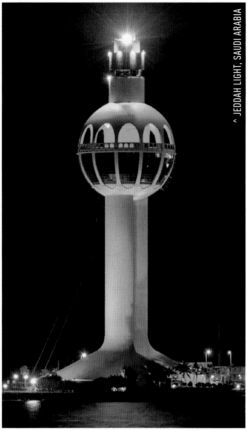

^ JEDDAH LIGHT, SAUDI ARABIA

IT'S A RECORD!

436 FEET

Jeddah Light (left), in Saudi Arabia, is the world's tallest lighthouse. It is built of steel and concrete and has nine elevators.

First Light

The Pharos of Alexandria was probably the world's first lighthouse. Built in Egypt in 280 BCE, it was one of the Seven Wonders of the Ancient World until it was damaged by earthquakes. Accounts from the time describe the lighthouse like this:

1823

In 1823, the first Fresnel lens was used in the Cordouan lighthouse in the Gironde estuary, France. It used angled glass pieces to bend and magnify light, and could be seen over 20 miles away.

BETWEEN 394–450 FT. TALL

A MIRROR REFLECTED SUN DURING THE DAY, AND A FLAME BURNED AT NIGHT

CYLINDRICAL SECTION

OCTAGONAL SECTION

SQUARE BASE, WITH SLOPING SIDES

IT STOOD ON THE ISLAND OF PHAROS IN THE HARBOR OF ALEXANDRIA, EGYPT

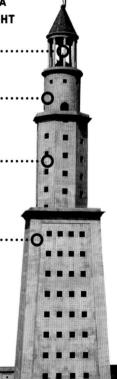

THIRD TIME'S A CHARM

The third lighthouse built on the Eddystone Reef, in 1756, changed lighthouse design altogether. The structure was strengthened by its curved shape and a base of massive granite blocks that dovetailed together.

UNBELIEVABLE BRIDGES

Bridges must support heavy loads, and they often span long distances over water or difficult terrain, making them very demanding engineering projects. But engineers have some amazing solutions to these tricky problems.

AKASHI KAIKYO BRIDGE

When it opened in 1998, this was the longest, tallest, and most expensive suspension bridge ever built. It hangs over the turbulent waters of the Akashi Strait, which connects Japan's mainland to the island of Awaji.

KOBE, JAPAN

FACT FILE

▲ Two ferries sank in the Akashi Strait during the same storm in 1955, highlighting the need for a bridge.

▲ Weather in the area is treacherous, with rainfall of up to 57 inches per year.

▲ There's also a danger of hurricanes, tsunamis, and earthquakes.

▲ The bridge is built to withstand winds of up to 180 mph and earthquakes with a magnitude of up to 8.5 on the Richter scale.

▲ Mechanized counterweights in the towers swing in the opposite direction when the wind blows, balancing the bridge.

928 FT.-TALL SUPPORTING TOWERS

THERE ARE 6 LANES OF TRAFFIC—OVER 23,000 CARS CROSS THE BRIDGE EVERY DAY

THE CENTRAL SPAN IS 6,532 FT. WIDE, WHICH IS WIDER THAN THE ORIGINAL DESIGN, AFTER AN EARTHQUAKE DURING CONSTRUCTION FORCED THE TWO TOWERS FARTHER APART

THE BRIDGE SPANS A TOTAL DISTANCE OF 12,831 FT.

Three hundred years before Europeans began to build suspension bridges, the Inca people of Peru were weaving them from grass, cotton, and llama wool! Some of the bridges spanned over 150 ft. and crossed deep gorges.

^ PONT DU GARD, FRANCE

2,000 YEARS OLD

The Pont du Gard is one of the oldest bridges in the world. It is part of a 31-mile-long aqueduct built by the Romans to carry water to the town of NÎmes, France. It has three levels, with the top level carrying the water.

FOUR MAIN BRIDGE TYPES

BEAM BRIDGE

1. Flexible deck

2. Supported by strong pillars

ARCH BRIDGE

1. The arch gives strength

2. Weight transfers to supporting pillars

CANTILEVER BRIDGE

1. Two trusses joined in middle by a suspended section

2. Each truss is supported at one end by a pier

3. Weight of bridge transfers to the piers

SUSPENSION BRIDGE

1. Suspender cables support deck

2. Towers support main cable

3. Weight transfers to concrete anchors secured in the ground

Canada's Quebec Bridge collapsed twice during construction, in 1907 and 1916! Despite the many deaths that occurred due to design and equipment failure, the bridge opened in 1919, and it's still the largest cantilever bridge in the world.

 186,000 miles of wire were used to make the Akashi Kaikyo's main cables—it could circle the Earth 7.5 times!

WITH A ROAD LEVEL OVER 200 FT. ABOVE SEA LEVEL, THE BRIDGE DOESN'T GET IN THE WAY OF SHIPPING BELOW

STRONG TRUSSES WITH TRIANGULAR BRACES KEEP THE BRIDGE RIGID, BUT LET THE WIND BLOW THROUGH

THE CABLES WERE CONNECTED BY HELICOPTER

IT'S A RECORD!

102 MILES LONG

The longest bridge in the world is the Danyang–Kunshan Grand Bridge (right) between Shanghai and Beijing. It crosses rice fields, a river delta, and open water.

^ DANYANG–KUNSHAN GRAND BRIDGE

*7 OF THE **WORLD'S** TOP 10 **LONGEST** BRIDGES CAN BE FOUND IN CHINA.*

AMAZING METROS

Since the first underground line was built in London in 1863, subway systems have opened in major cities around the world, and they're getting longer and busier all the time.

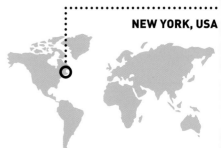

NEW YORK, USA

NEW YORK SUBWAY

When the New York subway system opened in 1904, over 100,000 people came along for the ride. It runs 24 hours a day, 365 days a year, and each year it carries around 1.75 billion passengers.

🤖 FACT FILE

◢ It took close to 8,000 workers to build the original New York subway tunnels.

◢ The positions of the tunnels were often aligned with the roads above ground, so traffic had to stop as the workers started digging.

◢ The tunnels are fairly close to the surface because the rock deeper down is too hard to cut.

◢ Steel and concrete piles helped to support the tunnels, while beams and trusses shaped the roof.

◢ The tunnels had to be covered with layers of concrete, asphalt, and felt, which would make them waterproof.

◢ There were 16 reported deaths during construction.

◢ After Superstorm Sandy hit New York in 2012, 600 million gallons of storm water had to be pumped out of the tunnels.

469

New York subway has 469 subway stations, more than any other city in the world!

TIME *TRIAL*

IT'S A RECORD!

Set in January 2015, the record for the fastest time to travel to every single New York subway station is: 21 hours, 49 minutes, and 35 seconds.

Underground Palaces

Moscow Metro (below) is one of the world's most beautiful underground systems. Designed to impress, the stations feature sweeping arches, chandeliers, murals, statues, and even stained-glass windows.

^ MOSCOW METRO

NUMBER *OF PASSENGERS*
*NUMBER OF PASSENGERS EACH YEAR

1. **BEIJING**—3.41 BILLION
2. **TOKYO**—3.22 BILLION
3. **SEOUL**—2.56 BILLION
4. **MOSCOW**—2.49 BILLION
5. **NEW YORK**—1.75 BILLION
6. **LONDON**—1.7 BILLION
7. **PARIS**—1.53 BILLION

MILES *OF TRACK*

1. **SEOUL**—584 MILES
2. **BEIJING**—327 MILES
3. **LONDON**—249 MILES
4. **NEW YORK**—229 MILES
5. **MOSCOW**—204 MILES
6. **TOKYO**—192 MILES
7. **PARIS**—130 MILES

Seoul's subway system is the longest in the world, and one of the best! Seoul's trains have wireless and 4G on board, and the seats heat up automatically when it's cold.

346 FEET DEEP

Kiev's Arsenalna metro station is the deepest in the world, avoiding the Dnieper River. Descending to the station platform takes a full 5 minutes down several escalators.

^ SEOUL METROPOLITAN SUBWAY

BELOW **THE METRO**

Workers digging tunnels for the Paris Metro found cannonballs, human bones, and Roman quarries underground! In order to cut through some of the sloppy mud, they froze it with calcium chloride.

^ TUNNEL BORING MACHINE

UP-TO-DATE **UNDERGROUND**

Today, a tunnel-boring machine (left) removes and crushes rock to create a tunnel; its cylindrical shape supports the tunnel as it digs. Concrete can be sprayed on the walls to finish them off.

METRO

 STUNNING STATUES

Over the centuries, statues have been placed in some breathtaking sites. These amazing monuments are incredible feats of human achievement.

LESHAN, SICHUAN, CHINA

BIGGEST BUDDHA

The Leshan Buddha is the biggest stone statue of Buddha in the world. He sits in a beautiful location in the Sichuan province of China, looking down on a point where three rivers meet.

🤖 FACT FILE

▲ Work on the statue began in 713 CE and went on for a full 90 years.

▲ The Buddha was carved out of the sandstone rock that surrounds him.

▲ The statue is 233 ft. tall, and the Buddha's head is often in the clouds.

▲ Workers started from the top of his head and cut down to his feet. That way no scaffolding was necessary.

▲ The ears remind followers of the privileged life Buddha gave up. The lobes are long because of the jeweled earrings he once wore.

▲ Gray patches on the statue's face and body are caused by acid rain—China has a serious pollution problem. Workers attached to ropes climb onto the statue to clean it.

250

A zigzagging path of over 250 narrow steps is cut into the rock so that people can climb up to the top of Buddha's head and take in the magnificent view of the statue.

^ MOUNT RUSHMORE, USA

2,310 FEET ABOVE SEA LEVEL

‹‹‹‹‹‹‹‹‹‹‹‹‹‹

Christ the Redeemer watches over Rio de Janeiro in Brazil. The statue is 98 ft. tall and stands on top of a 26 ft. plinth. People can look up from any point in the city and see the 700-ton statue.

PRESIDENTS' ROCK

Mount Rushmore in South Dakota's Black Hills National Forest is the site of four massive carved sculptures of four US presidents.

◢ 450,000 tons of rock was blasted to create the monument, which was completed in 1941.

◢ 400 workers built the monument, hanging from cables over the 500-foot-tall rock face. Following scale models, workers used dynamite to blast the rock, ready for carving. A honeycomb of holes was drilled to specific depths before the rock was "bumped," or smoothed, and the features chiseled by hand.

◢ The granite of Mount Rushmore erodes at a rate of 1 in. per 100,000 years—that's hard rock! Scientists estimate that the faces will be visible for around 100,000 years.

IT'S A RECORD!

715 FEET TALL

The world's largest stone carving is in the Meng Shan mountains, China, and shows the Chinese god of long life.

900 STATUES

›››››››››››

The approx. number of statues on Easter Island (right). The largest is 33 ft. tall.

^ EASTER ISLAND

LAVISH PALACES

Palaces are often started by one important person, then extended, redesigned, and rebuilt by later generations. They range from the simple and stylish to the downright over-the-top!

BUCKINGHAM PALACE

It's been the official London home of the British royal family since Queen Victoria moved here in 1837.

 FACT FILE

◣ The palace started out as a country house, in 1703.

◣ George III bought it in 1761 for his family home. New sections were added over the centuries.

◣ Inside, the ballroom is the largest of the 775 rooms, measuring 120 feet long. The kitchens can serve up to 600 people.

◣ There's also a post office, chapel, swimming pool, staff canteen, and movie theater.

◣ The palace has the largest privately owned gardens in London and features a lake, tennis courts, and a helipad.

LONDON, UK

THE BEST-KNOWN SIDE OF THE PALACE WAS THE LAST SECTION TO BE BUILT, IN THE 1840S, AND THE WHITE PORTLAND STONE FRONT WAS ADDED IN 1913, REPLACING A DIRTY BLACK FAÇADE CAUSED BY POLLUTION

POSSIBLY THE MOST FAMOUS BALCONY IN THE WORLD. THE FIRST ROYAL APPEARANCE ON HERE WAS IN 1851.

354 FT. LON
79 FT. TAL

WRITING ON THE WALL

It took Spanish Muslims centuries to build the Alhambra. Islamic art uses geometric patterns and script rather than human images, so these were used to decorate the palace walls. Mathematicians still study the geometry of the architecture and the décor today.

IT'S A RECORD!

LARGEST RESIDENTIAL PALACE

Istana Nurul Iman in Brunei was completed in 1984 and occupies 2,152,782 sq. ft. It boasts 1,788 rooms, a banquet hall for 5,000 people, five swimming pools, and a garage for 110 cars.

Cliff Palace

In 1200 CE, around 100 people lived in the Mesa Verde Cliff Palace, built in an alcove in the sandstone in Colorado, USA. Entering via wooden ladders, they occupied 150 brightly plastered rooms and held ceremonies in round rooms, called "kivas."

LIGHT *FANTASTIC*

The Palace of Versailles (below) started out as a hunting lodge in 1624, then became an extravagant palace and gardens for the French royal family. 3,000 ministers, courtiers, and servants lived here in 350 apartments. The 240-foot-long Hall of Mirrors could be the most famous room in the world. It has:

- ◢ 17 mirrored arches
- ◢ 17 huge windows
- ◢ 32 vast ceiling paintings glorifying the king
- ◢ 357 mirrors in total (luxury items at the time)
- ◢ Many chandeliers and statues, and lots of gold!

THE FORECOURT, GATES, AND RAILINGS WERE ADDED IN 1911, IN MEMORY OF QUEEN VICTORIA

 Rumor has it a secret tunnel connects the palace to the Houses of Parliament.

THE PALACE'S 760 WINDOWS ARE CLEANED EVERY SIX WEEKS

^ HALL OF MIRRORS, VERSAILLES

8,886 *ROOMS*

That's how many rooms are in the Imperial Palace in Beijing, China—the largest palace in the world. Work on its 980 buildings finished in 1420; it took more than 1,000,000 workers to complete them.

🗼 INCREDIBLE EXCAVATION

People have been mining underground for thousands of years, so as reserves of different minerals run low, the mines are getting deeper.

MPONENG, SOUTH AFRICA

DEEP DOWN GOLD

Mponeng in South Africa is the deepest mine in the world. In fact, eight out of the world's 10 deepest mines are in South Africa, and they're all gold mines: 50% of the world's known gold deposits lie under the area around Johannesburg.

TUNNELS, CALLED CROSSCUTS, ARE NARROW TO AVOID TOO MUCH STRESS ON THE ROCK ABOVE

EACH 4-FT. PILLA
MAY BE SUPPORTIN
10 TONS OF ROC

🤖 FACT FILE

◢ The Mponeng mine is the world's most dangerous construction project.

◢ Blasting farther into the rock causes daily earth tremors.

◢ 15,000 lb. of rock have to be excavated to produce just 100 lb. of solid gold. The gold looks like tiny powdery flecks in the rock.

◢ It takes over an hour to get to the very deepest section of the mine.

236 MILES

The length of the mine tunnels in Mponeng—that's about the size of the New York subway system!

4,000 PEOPLE WORK HERE EVERY DAY

6,000 TONS OF ROCK ARE EXTRACTED EACH DAY, AND THE SEAM OF ORE IS ONLY 30 IN. WIDE

^ KIMBERLEY, SOUTH AFRICA

ROUGH DIAMONDS

Kimberley, South Africa, has one of the deepest open-cast mines (with no tunnels or shafts) in the world. The Big Hole was dug approximately 790 ft. down, to excavate diamonds, using only picks and shovels.

OLDEST

The remains of a mine around 43,000 years old exist in Swaziland. The red ocher excavated there was sprinkled on dead bodies during burial ceremonies.

GOLDEN GIANT

Muruntau in Uzbekistan is the world's largest open-cast gold mine, producing 2.6 million ounces of gold in 2014.

2 MILES *LONG*
1.4 MILES *WIDE*
1,968 FT. *DEEP*

❄ 140°F

The temperature at the bottom of Mponeng is 140°F. Snow machines at the surface pump ice and salt into the tunnels. Fans blowing over the mixture bring the temperature down to 85°F.

46 FEET *PER SECOND*

The approximate speed of Mponeng's triple-decker lift. It can hold up to 120 people and takes 6 minutes to descend 1.6 miles.

IT'S A RECORD!

1.94 MILES LONG

The length of the world's longest single-shaft lift in Moab Khotsong Gold mine, South Africa.

69 *DAYS*

The longest period miners have survived underground. In 2010, 33 men were hauled out alive, having been trapped 2,297 ft. down the San José mine, Chile.

IT'S IN THE PIPELINE

Pipelines have been a useful way of transporting large volumes of liquid for millennia. They're a fantastic engineering achievement, but when a pipe leaks, the environment suffers.

TRANS-ALASKA PIPELINE

(Below) This is one of the largest pipeline systems in the world, carrying crude oil from the Arctic Ocean to the port of Valdez, Alaska, at a distance of 800 miles.

 The oil takes around 5.5 days to reach its destination.

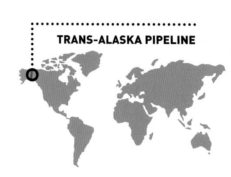

TRANS-ALASKA PIPELINE

 **FACT FILE**

◢ Oil was discovered at Prudhoe Bay, Alaska, in 1968, and construction on the pipeline started in 1975.

◢ Prudhoe is North America's largest oil field and provides 20 percent of US oil.

◢ Because the Arctic Ocean here is only ice-free for 6 weeks of the year, the oil has to be transported to the milder port of Valdez. Here, it is loaded onto supertankers and shipped to oil refineries.

◢ The pipe is monitored from a control center in Valdez, but there are also pump stations along the route.

THE PIPELINE INCLUDES 554 ARCHES WITH A MINIMUM HEIGHT OF 10 FT., ALLOWING CARIBOU AND OTHER WILDLIFE TO PASS UNDER IT ON THEIR TRAILS

78,000 SUPPORTS LIKE THIS ONE ARE PLACED 60 FT. APART

OVER 50 PERCENT OF THE PIPELIN IS ABOVE GROUND BECAUSE BURYIN THE PIPES IN THE WRONG CONDITION COULD CAUSE THE GROUND TO THA AND PIPES TO SIN

1.5 MILLION

BARRELS A DAY

The amount of oil produced in one day at Prudhoe Bay at its peak in 1988. In over 25 years, it has produced over 12 billion barrels.

4.5 MILLION TONS

The amount of crude oil spilled on land in Russia every year due to poor pipe maintenance and extreme weather conditions.

THE ZIGZAG IN THE PIPELINE HELPS IT RESIST EARTHQUAKES, AND THE PIPE IS DESIGNED TO MOVE UP TO 5 FT. VERTICALLY AND 20 FT. HORIZONTALLY

What a Gas!

Russia supplies gas to Turkey via the Blue Stream pipeline, which tunnels through mountains and runs under the Black Sea. The pipeline is 754 miles long and submerged to a depth that's over 2.5 times the height of the Burj Khalifa—the world's tallest building.

1.4 MILES

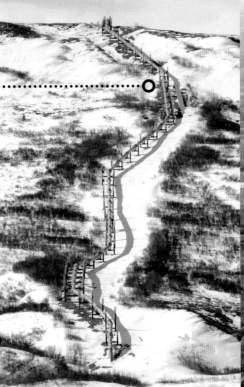

3,728 MILES

The length of gas pipeline lying at the bottom of the North Sea.

PIPES IN THE PAST

◣ Bamboo pipes were used to carry water in China in 5,000 BCE.

◣ Egyptians were using copper pipes around 3,000–4,000 BCE.

◣ Early civilizations carried water via aqueducts. Some Roman aqueducts still survive today.

◣ Most pipes were made of stone, wood, clay, or lead, until cast iron became a cheap alternative in the eighteenth century.

◣ The first oil pipeline was laid in Pennsylvania in 1865. It covered a distance of 5 miles and cut the cost of transporting oil hugely, making it much cheaper.

IT'S A RECORD!

2,353 MILES

The longest crude oil pipeline in the world runs 2,353 miles, from Alberta, Canada, to Chicago, USA, and back to Montreal in Canada.

JUST FOR FUN

As theme parks get bigger, the rides grow too, which makes the jobs of designing, engineering, and maintaining them even more difficult. Having fun can be a very serious business!

FERRARI WORLD

Ferrari World in Abu Dhabi is the largest indoor amusement park on Earth. Fully air-conditioned inside, it offers visitors over 20 spectacular rides, all based around Ferrari cars. The roof is 2,297 feet wide.

ABU DHABI, UAE

? *Turned on its side, Ferrari World would be the tallest man-made structure on the planet and a whopping 300 floors high!*

FACT FILE

▲ Ferrari World opened in 2010, just in time for the Formula 1 Grand Prix in Abu Dhabi.

▲ Over 12,000 tons of steel was used to build the roof, which is supported by 12 columns positioned in the shape of an Arabic star.

▲ It took just over one year to construct the roof and two years to complete the park.

▲ The building is only three floors high. The roof had to stay low because of the airport nearby.

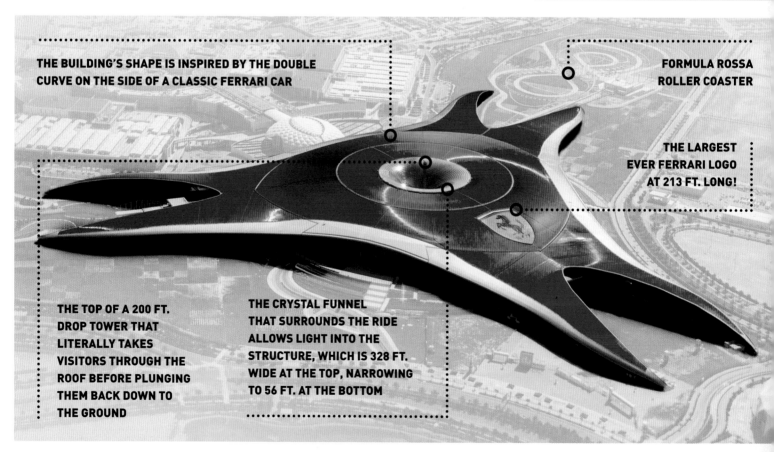

THE BUILDING'S SHAPE IS INSPIRED BY THE DOUBLE CURVE ON THE SIDE OF A CLASSIC FERRARI CAR

FORMULA ROSSA ROLLER COASTER

THE LARGEST EVER FERRARI LOGO AT 213 FT. LONG!

THE TOP OF A 200 FT. DROP TOWER THAT LITERALLY TAKES VISITORS THROUGH THE ROOF BEFORE PLUNGING THEM BACK DOWN TO THE GROUND

THE CRYSTAL FUNNEL THAT SURROUNDS THE RIDE ALLOWS LIGHT INTO THE STRUCTURE, WHICH IS 328 FT. WIDE AT THE TOP, NARROWING TO 56 FT. AT THE BOTTOM

CITY-SIZED

Disney World opened in 1971, and it's still the largest amusement park in the world. The whole resort is as big as the city of San Francisco, USA!

Here are a few facts about its iconic Cinderella's Castle attraction:

◢ It was inspired by French châteaux and a church in Prague.

◢ It contains no bricks. It's built of steel and concrete, with a plaster finish.

◢ It is 189 feet tall, but with its 27 towers, the design tricks you into thinking the castle is much taller.

^ DISNEY WORLD, FLORIDA

^ FORMULA ROSSA, FERRARI WORLD

IT'S A RECORD!

150 MPH

The Formula Rossa ride (above) at Ferrari World is the world's fastest roller coaster, whipping riders out into the desert heat at speeds of up to 150 mph.

ROLLER COASTER
SAFETY
US ROLLER COASTER SAFETY STATS 2013

Chance of serious injury on a roller coaster

= 1 IN 24 MILLION

Chance of fatal injury on a roller coaster

= 1 IN 750 MILLION

Chance of injury while playing football

= 450 IN 1 MILLION

Chance of injury while camping

= 5 IN 1 MILLION

Chance of being struck by lightning

= 1 IN 775,000

BIG DROP

The Sky Drop on China's Canton Tower is the highest thrill ride in the world, lifting riders part of the way up the antenna at the tip of the building before dropping them over 98 ft. in less than 2 seconds. The tower also has the world's highest Ferris wheel.

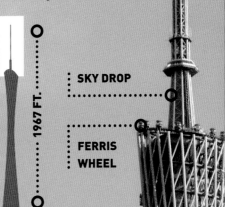

1967 FT.

SKY DROP

FERRIS WHEEL

FLYING HIGH

As more and more people take to the skies, the world's airports and airplanes are having to expand and adapt—and consider the environment.

BEIJING INTERNATIONAL AIRPORT

When Terminal 3 opened in Beijing in 2008, it was the world's most advanced airport, the largest building in the world, and the first with a volume of over 3,280,839 cubic feet.

BEIJING, CHINA

THE ROOF'S CURVE GIVES MORE SPACE INSIDE THE BUILDING

PLENTY OF GLASS MEANS THE BUILDING HAS NATURAL LIGHT THROUGHOUT

50 *MILLION*
PASSENGERS A YEAR

The number of passengers the terminal expects to accommodate by 2020.

 FACT FILE

◢ The new terminal was completed in 2008, just in time for the Beijing Olympics. It took just four years to build.

◢ It may be huge, but color-coding, among other design features, makes finding your way around easy.

◢ The length of the building from north to south is just over 2 miles, but passengers can travel between sections by "people mover" in just 2 minutes.

◢ It is one of the world's most environmentally sustainable airports. Local materials and local workers were used on the build, and energy consumption is carefully controlled.

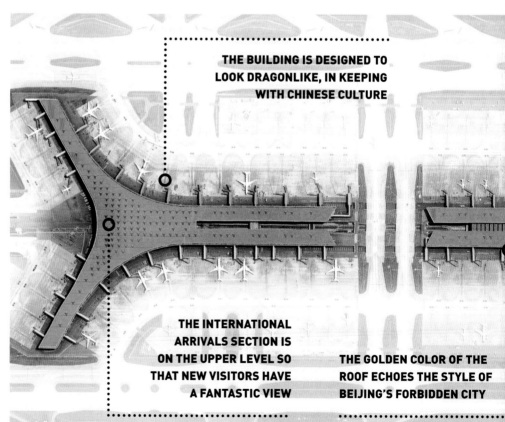

THE BUILDING IS DESIGNED TO LOOK DRAGONLIKE, IN KEEPING WITH CHINESE CULTURE

THE INTERNATIONAL ARRIVALS SECTION IS ON THE UPPER LEVEL SO THAT NEW VISITORS HAVE A FANTASTIC VIEW

THE GOLDEN COLOR OF THE ROOF ECHOES THE STYLE OF BEIJING'S FORBIDDEN CITY

2014 AIRPORT RECORDS

«««««««««

WORLD'S BUSIEST AIRPORT
Atlanta, USA = 96 million passengers

MOST INTERNATIONAL PASSENGERS
Dubai, UAE = nearly 70 million passengers

MOST CARGO TRAFFIC
Hong Kong = 4,867,788 tons of cargo loaded and unloaded

MOST FLIGHTS
Chicago O'Hare, USA = 881,933 takeoffs and landings

^ BARAJAS AIRPORT, SPAIN

Color-coded
Madrid's Barajas International Airport has a stunning wavelike ceiling. It is made from sustainable bamboo and supported by colored pillars that match the boarding passes—so it's easy to figure out which way to go.

PREFLIGHT ENTERTAINMENT

Passing a few hours in Changi Airport, Singapore, is never a problem. There's a rooftop swimming pool, movie theater, gardens, and a games center with Xboxes and Playstations.

^ CHANGI AIRPORT, SINGAPORE

RADITIONAL CHINESE COLORS OF
ED, ORANGE, AND YELLOW ARE
SED INSIDE THE BUILDING, WHICH
 DESIGNED TO BE PEACEFUL AND
ELCOMING

HE SKYLIGHTS ARE DESIGNED
 BRING IN THE WARMTH OF THE
INTER SUN AND TO KEEP OUT THE
XTREME SUMMER HEAT

KEEP IT DOWN!

Air traffic produces 2% of the world's carbon emissions. Every 5.5-lb. saving in the weight of a plane results in a 1-ton reduction in carbon emissions.

2🌎57
ZERO-EMISSIONS

»»»»»»»

The year it's hoped the first zero-emissions planes will be flying our skies.

GLOSSARY

ABSEILER Someone who uses ropes to lower themselves down a steep-sided structure

AFTERLIFE Ancient Egyptians believed they had another life after they died

AMPHITHEATER Circular building with a stage in the middle for entertainment

AQUEDUCT A structure for transporting water

ARENA Area with seating around it, where sports games or entertainment take place

ARRAY (SOLAR) A collection of solar panels arranged to catch the most sunlight

ASSASSINATION Murder for political or religious reasons

ASTRONOMY The study of space and the universe

AWNING A fabric shelter supported by a frame

BANKRUPTCY When a person has no money left to pay off their debts

BANQUET A formal meal with a large group of people

BLACK DEATH A deadly plague that spread through Europe in the fourteenth century

BUBONIC PLAGUE An often deadly infection caught from fleas carried by rats. The Black Death was an outbreak of bubonic plague.

CANAL LOCKS A device used for raising and lowering boats and ships between stretches of water of different levels on canal waterways

CHASSIS The wheeled frame that supports the body of a vehicle

CIRCUMFERENCE The measurement around the outside of a circle

CLADDING A protective covering on the outside of a structure

COMPOUND (PULLEY) Combining a fixed and movable pulley to make it easier to move a large object

CONCENTRIC Circles which have the same central point

COUNTERWEIGHT A weight used to balance another similar-sized weight

CULTIVATE To grow plants under controlled conditions

CUPOLA A round dome on top of a roof

CYLINDRICAL In the shape of a cylinder

DUO A pair

DYNASTY A family of kings or rulers who rule for many generations

EMPEROR A man in charge of an empire

EMPIRE A group of countries with one ruler

FESTOONED Decorated with a chain (of flowers)

GARRISON A military camp

GLADIATOR A man trained to fight other men in a Roman arena

GRANITE A very hard type of rock

GREEN TIMBER Newly cut wood that still contains a lot of moisture

HYDRAULIC Operated by a liquid moving in a confined space under pressure

KNOTS Measure of speed for a ship or aircraft

LABORATORY A building or room used to carry out scientific experiments

LATIN AMERICA Countries to the south of the USA, where French, Spanish, or Portuguese are spoken

LIMESTONE A rock used as a building material, and in cement

MAGNITUDE Greatness of size

MICROGRAVITY Weak gravity, for example in a spacecraft in orbit

MING A Chinese dynasty that ruled from the fourteenth to seventeenth centuries

MOAT A ditch, often filled with water, that surrounds a castle as a form of defense

MODULE One separate part that can be joined with others to make a larger structure

MORTAR A mixture used to hold bricks together in a building

MULE A small electric vehicle that can pull or guide a larger vehicle

PILE A vertical structural element of a deep foundation, driven into the ground at the building site

PHARAOH A ruler of ancient Egypt

PHYSICIST A scientist who studies physics

PULLEY A simple machine consisting of a wheel over which a pulled rope or chain runs. Two or more pulleys work together to reduce the force needed to lift a load (see compound pulley).

QIN A Chinese dynasty that ruled in the 3rd century BCE

SATELLITE A man-made piece of equipment placed in orbit around the Earth, Moon, or another planet to collect information or for communication

SCAFFOLD A temporary structure used by workers during the erection, repair, or decoration of a building

SCUBA DIVING A kind of underwater diving where the diver uses a self-contained underwater breathing apparatus (scuba) to breathe underwater

TELESCOPIC Having tubular sections which are designed to slide into one another

TOLL A charge made for use of a bridge, canal, or other crossing

TRUSS A main support of a structure

UNESCO United Nations Educational Scientific and Cultural Organization

WEEVIL A small beetle that infests crops

WORLD WAR II A war fought from 1939 to 1945 between the Axis powers—Germany, Italy, and Japan—and the Allies, which included France and Britain, and later the Soviet Union and the United States

INDEX

ACKNOWLEDGMENTS

PICTURE CREDITS:

KEY—tl top left, **tc** top center, **tr** top right, **cl** center left, **c** center, **cr** center right, **bl** bottom left, **bc** bottom center, **br** bottom right.

© **Shutterstock:** 4b Aitormmfoto, 4tr TILT Photography, 4tl meunierd, 4bl Frederic Legrand - COMEO, 10c Computer Earth, 11bc Aitormmfoto, 13t TILT Photography, 19cl Nelosa, 20c Martchan, 20tr OPIS Zagreb, 21br Anthony Shaw Photography, 22c KalypsoWorldPhotography, 26bl Zigzag Mountain Art, 27cr andrej pol, 27bc Everett Historical, 29tr Migel, 29br Nattika, 30c TonyV3112, 30bl TonyV3112, 31cl Nightman1965, 32c Adrian Hughes, 33c meunierd, 36c CJM Grafx, 37tr Thor Jorgen Udvang, 39br Zhukov Oleg, 40c Javen, 42c Stephen B. Goodwin, 39br BORTEL Pavel - Pavelmidi, 44c twoKim, 44bl Smit, 45tr Robert St-Coeur, 46c pisaphotography, 47tl Viacheslav Lopatin, 47bl PI, 47c meunierd, 47br Netfalls - Remy Musser, 48c lzf, 49bl AAR Studio, 49tr dmitry_islentev, 50c r.nagy, 51tl Shchipkova Elena, 51br Frederic Legrand - COMEO, 56c Burachet, 57cr Patryk Kosmider, 58tl Tooykrub

© **istock:** 4c Supannee_Hickman, 4br takepicsforfun, 6c spinka, 7cr Noppasin Wongchum, 7bl sihasakprachum, 8c EnginKorkmaz, 9cb katherinejoline, 9tc Supannee_Hickman, 12tr HackneyKate, 12b pierivb, 14c takepicsforfun, 15tl CircleEyes, 15c Martchan, 15b David4real, 16c scaliger, 17tl zhaojiankang, 17tr steffie82, 18bc Dan77, 18tc Marco Regalia, 19c vovashevchuk, 19cr aphotostory, 23cr tonefotografia, 26c onlymehdi, 31cr donvictorio, 35c 3DSculptor, 37cl mazzzur, 37br Piero Cruciatti, 38c Gala98, 39tl CoDuck, 39bl joetamassy, 41c jackchen52000, 41br photoquest7, 41tr iSailorr, 43tc IgorSPb, 44bc sigurcamp, 45bc Xieyouding, 49tc karenparker2000, 49br Vladimir_Krupenkin, 53tr bmyl2, 53cr Robin372, 54c kyletperry, 55cb helt2, 57tr Aneese, 57vr xcctfsi, 59tc Meinzahn, 59cr bayuharsa

© **Getty Images:** 52c Bloomberg, 58cb DigitalGlobe/ScapeWare © **Alamy Stock Photo:** 28c WENN Ltd

© **CERN:** 24c, 25cb CERN © **NASA:** 34c, 35cb © **Wikimedia Commons:** 43cl Henry Whinstanley

All other vector art © Shutterstock, © istock and Dynamo Limited